FLASHES FROM MY PAST:

KING AMONG THE PRAWNS

TIM HIGGINS

I wrote a fair number of poems in my younger days, saved and placed in a folder titled "King Among the Prawns". Now that I'm self-publishing my more recent books, I decided to let these out for a ramble.

Some of them I'm quite proud of, and some are fairly naff. They exist as windows on a time in my life when I was naïve but learning. Along with these are a second batch, inspired by the trauma and after effects of my brain haemorrhage and stroke in 2009, and a mental health poetry group I was introduced to shortly after my stroke; great therapy! A few were published in their anthologies.

Some of the things I wrote I still cling to, some I have discarded now as I have gained in age. Many of us would wish to sit down with our younger self and have a good talk, wouldn't we? [Audiobook of me reading out my own poems will follow at some point].

Other books:

Some Words of Mine (and a few quotes) - self-published on Amazon and Kindle, and audiobook on Audible.

The Greatest Sermon Ever Preached - self-published on Amazon and Kindle, audiobook to follow.

In the pipeline:

The Fall of Ananias & Sapphira

The Obsidian Way of Jesus; Through a Glass, Darkly

Subscribe to my blog and/or my YouTube channel to get news on this and future blogs/ vlogs/ books…

www.thealternativeulsterman.com
'The Alternative Ulsterman' channel on YouTube

Contents

x

SAND

In the sand I wrote, a face I drew
To tell the world what my heart knew
One of the things I count as true.

Knowing that within the day
The tide would turn and wash away
The candid disclosure I could not say.

Was this the whole, the full-blown truth?
Discovered, emerging from my youth.
Now thirty, my novice wisdom uncouth.

For the sand does shift, it comes and goes
With no volition in the ebbs and flows
And no ambition to interpose
Any objection to the merciless tide
Its arranged, surrendered, unwilling bride
In whom only a fool would dare confide.

Since the sea shall sequester every script
And drag it out to its ranging crypt
'Til all intent from its spirit is stripped.

Then devoid and vacant, without worth,
Thrown back to where it had its birth
But strewn across a wider girth.

Taking my stick, I wrote more words
Only to be seen by passing birds
And solely by the breeze to be heard.

Hoping that this other fact
Would be taken by the sea intact
Added to the first in pact
And someday to my world brought back.

Belief, unless by rock is breached
Will meld with other grains of beach.
Then other truths will come along
And together write another song.

Portsalon, Lough Swilly, County Donegal.
18/5/95.

THE HIGH PLACE

Now I've climbed the mountain
There's nowhere left to go
Except down to the valley
From the high back to the low.

If the wind is against me
The job will be just worse
But if it is behind me
It will simply be a curse.

For I'd rather stay on the top all day
Than return to what I know.

Slieve League, Donegal.
13/7/95.

THREE CLERIHEWS

[A clerihew is a whimsical, four-line biographical poem invented by Edmund Clerihew Bentley. The first line is the name of the poem's subject, usually a famous person put in an absurd light, or revealing something unknown or spurious about them. The rhyme scheme is AABB, and the rhymes are often forced.] - Wikipedia

Jeremy Paxman
is known to be deadpan,
But this can bely
how his humour is dry.

Stephen Hawking
has difficulty talking.
But never mind,
his brain is just fine.

Gordon Brown
has a terrible frown.
But his attempt at a smile
is worse by a mile!

18/9/09.

CENTRE

At the centre of our sky, of our space
Stands a star, brightly shining
A fixed beacon, always North.
Pointing the way for all to follow,
Towards their hope and onto rest,
Saving the lost and guiding home.

All other lights circle in reverence
As if bowed to its stately balance.
Centre of a universe of ebony,
Set stone in a realm of diamonds.
Composite beauty of thousands
Hinges on the simplicity of one.

At the centre of history, of our time
Stands a cross, darkly brooding,
A fixed event, always present.
Showing the One whom all must follow
To their death, then onto life
Saving the lost and leading home.

All other events circle in deference
Kneeling humbly to the prime importance.
Centre of a universe of misery,
Blessed Hope in a sea of injury.
Created beauty of billions
Reflect the conception of one.

7/11/95.

MOON

On a light wind-whisked night
The moon's light shines bright
Frighteningly white, cold as tight-packed snow.

The clouds fly in shrouds
And 'round her crown crowd
Bowed and avowed to her proud halo.

How they chase 'cross her face
Interlace in their grace
Pacing with haste, they trace out shadows.

I'm sold to her hold
Cold as rolled gold
Scrolled in their folds she boldly glows.

My will and wish still
Is to be filled with the thrill
Shrill in the chill that she drills through my soul.

Lagan Towpath, Drumbeg
10/10/95.

LEMON

Lemon colour
Brilliant summer
Bitter after-taste.

Rain flails down
This soggy town
The sun shoved off with haste.

LIFE TRILOGY:

A DAY I'LL NEVER FORGET

How blessed I am!
We are.
How blessed we are indeed!
So many lost so much
So many times.
Yet that day,
despite my wife's berserk call,
the manic moment,
the furious drive from work to the hospital,
the beseeching petitions to heaven,
she was fine.
Our daughter had not drowned.

A DAY I'LL NEVER REMEMBER

The seizures came so suddenly.
Standing in church
Then the paramedic.
Then the ambulance;
its vaguely darkened windows.
Nothing more.
"They *had* to sedate you,"
a friend told me later.
Think I lashed out at some poor nurses,
or is that an induced nightmare
like the seizures I only see
in those vile vagaries
of my mind's own incubus?
A whole day lost,
or two
or three
I've never really known!

GRASPING THE EDGE

Intensive Care Unit:
Monitor sounds, heat, low light,
Icky mask and taped feeding tube.
"No, no, leave that on!"
Endless questions-
Of course I knew the year,
and our Prime Minister.
I wasn't out that long, surely.

I knew it.
I scanned that valley,
Dark and brooding;
The one King David saw.
And felt the fear, the apprehension at least,
As I grasped its rugged edge.
A hand grasped mine and reassured me.
He took my fear
and threw it away.
I spoke with him, clearer than ever.
"Who'll look after Karen and the kids?"
"I will. You know that."
"OK. If it's my time, Lord, so be it"
Peace.

"But you know I want more time,
want to see my grandkids on my knee,
fulfil something of a destiny
you must have for me.
Though not like Hezekiah;
I will not plead.
If so, so be it!"

He reassures me again,
avows me more time.

Haze of silence over my wife's face,
espied through my half-closed eyes.
She smiles.

24/10/09.

FLASH

* * * *The flick of a meteor* * * *
* * * *Splitting the infinite black** * *
* * * * Is over in an instant* * -----**
* * *And cannot be brought back. * *
* * * * But before it entered * * * *
* * * * The domain of the Earth,* ** *
****It travelled a thousand lifetimes* *
* * ** From the place of its birth.*** *

Playing Fields, Dunmurry
16*8*95

11

DARKNESS

When the darkness falls
The moon has gone
And the stars behind the clouds are hid,
The angel calls
My spirit on
And my anxious fears to death are bid
But will I stand
Against the tide?
Will courage fail me at the test?
Or fate demand
That flight will bide
And put my skittish soul to rest?

How can I know
If I'll be strong
Before the day of judgement dawns.
Time will show
If I am wrong
To think I'm king among the pawns.
Through trying times
I'll have to learn
To learn from every trial I face
And face my crimes,
Those crimes that churn
Within my darkest, hidden place.

The greatest voyage,
It is said,
Has to start with the first step.
But this wise adage
Has conveyed

A truth which in our minds has slept.
To beat the rise
Of evil
In everything I see
I must surprise
The Devil
By seeing the sin in me.

Shanky's Hollow, Mourne Mountains
25/8/95.

SEED

They seek to change me; make me conform
To a pattern the fallen world has borne
Unsure of themselves, their hearts are blind
And originality they cannot find.

If our prudent God wished us all the same
He would have designed man without a brain
And when he made Adam, in those days of old
I'm sure he'd have decided to keep the one mould.

His second choice, Eve, was made from his flesh
And his intention was surely for their souls to mesh
But her singleness showed her own thoughts were as true
Did they always agree, or each keep to their own view?

But I find that those who repress others' self
Believe in the right to keep their own wealth
Strange how they often talk of accommodation
When to share in society is a forbidden vocation.

Artists, writers, musicians, orators
Are the ones first attacked by scared dictators
For those who express their one individuality
Sow the first seeds of freedom in the community.

Silly hats and party ties
Are all I see crowning the lies
That appearances are not just facade
And respectability is something to be had.

"To be had" is more apt a phrase
As some are drawn in their early days

When mastery of reason is but a seed
And the virgin soil spoiled by every creed.

Ruined subtilely by the plant of greed
Resembling not any other weed
For it bears tempting succulent fruit
But all evil springs from its root.

One's possession to another is theft
So the capitalist has nothing left.
On the principle of the widow's mite
A socialist forever will be my right.

20/8/95.

I LOVED YOU... WHEN?
(VALENTINE'S DAY 2010)

I loved you then; I love you now,
Though logic asks just why and how.
You do my head in, as I do yours
And we're incompatible; of that I'm sure.
I drink coffee, you drink tea
And I've so many books that you can't see
The walls of some of our rooms at home
And if I buy one more, you'll surely moan.

You'll ask what to wear, again and again
Till it goes way beyond merely causing me pain
And I'll just reply, "no comment, love"
Then you'll storm off, give that door a huge shove.
And those songs you sing, with the words all wrong;
How I wish we were on a show with a gong
So I could bang it, and see you go
And suffer the torture no more, but no!
You'd get your revenge the next time I'd snore;
Shove me in the ribs and knock me on the floor.

But despite all that, when all's said and done
I thank the Lord, that you don't have a gun!

No, I thank the Lord, that after 22 years,
We share everything: the laughter and the tears.

UNFAILING

These mountains are so vast,
So anchored yet so free.
Lying under sunrise, sunset,
And all that's in between.
The challenge of the scaling
Of the incline of the ground
Is my soul's solo calling,
Always skyward, homeward bound.

Clear morning air,
Cool dawning light,
Mellows the heather's woody coarse.
The warming stair
Of the sun's flight
Lightens and lathers rigour and gorse.

Climbing up their incline,
The brush of herb on boot.
The sphagnum squelch is strangely
Warm and soothing underfoot.
Rush of river's water,
Endless flux of roar,
Overlaying silence
Which the birdsong will restore.

Tight gasping breast,
Taut sinewed force
Power the drive to drive to the top.
Soon dawning crest
Of struggle's divorce
Romances my strive to unfail and not stop.

Mourne Mountains, 23/9/95.

WANDERER

I looked straight up, into the sky
And saw a satellite passing by
Whisking across the specks on soot
A beacon of life without any root.

Spinning silently, with no care
Yet sending its signals to who knows where
Or maybe the tin can has finished its task
And ploughs through the void as a funeral cask?

The speed it must move and the sights that it sees
I wonder if I could escape through the trees
To its solitary path 'round this glowing ball
Reflecting the sunlight, seen by all
Who would chance to look or care to espy
This occasional visitor to their piece of sky.

To fly through the nil and look down below
And marvel at creation's splendrous halo;
Mountains, deserts, forests in shrouds
Of wispy, fleeting and mingling clouds.

For perhaps a day, spinning blue and green
'Til I'd had enough of all that could be seen
For loneliness is unkind; while creative and pure
It can lead to thoughts, moods and feelings insecure.

My words may seem glib, my ponderings twee
But one of the truths experience shows me
Is that no man's an island, and though he may choose
To be a lone wanderer, he never must lose
Sight of the fact that if the satellite would pause,
It would blend with the pattern of the starry gauze.

Playing Fields, Dunmurry, 11/6/95.

PSYCHOPROCRASTINATION

Don't stop
thinking about tomorrow.

It's one sure way
of getting nothing done
today.

17/10/85.

GREEN & ORANGE

This land so green,
Will always plane out
In herbed plot,
To where earth rises
In heather darker,
In summer stained purple.
Sea of Tranquility.
Waves of stonerise,
Interspersed, intersect.
Constructed, construed
To mark off territory
And not yield an inch to the other side.
No surrender to the force of root or blade.

Swathes of windswept emerald succulence
Cover the world's baseness beneath.
'Cept where man chose to tear up this haven
And plough through restoration
Of the natural order
Of things
Intended for the harmony of the wholeness,
Bestowed on the macrocosmic genesis
Caressed by the first footsteps of Adam.

The Earth, made for us,
Is unmade by us, in the throes of our careless apathy.

These flames, so orange,
Roaring out ravage under heaven's silent gaze.
Gapes of building emanating belching
From mouths that devour their material meal.
Passionate tongues of volume,

Licking the soot back off the glistening roof
Of the night sky they have obscured
With an obscene of obsidian.
Dusty dark of destruction, disparate
From ebony of evening's enkindling
Of sparkling sugar-sprinkling of stars.

Worshippers gather 'round the pyre
In the tumult of their nocturnal rite.
Veneration of the deity of ruin,
Devastation, catastrophe, strewn
At the feet of this golden idol.
Exalting the flames higher,
They reach for greater pinnacles of depravity.
Vandalism their inspiration,
Debasement their creed,
Frenzy their high priest,
Entropy their belief.

Our false gods shall always be the same
And paradise nought but lore
Whispered to children 'fore their sweet sleep of dreams.

Mourne Mountains & Dunmurry
12th & 13th July 1996.

SOON ONLY BEAUTY

Beauty and the Beast
Lie together in my soul
In uneasy peace
Discordant within the whole.
The hand of the creator
Can be seen in all this strife
If the sun of his colour
Paints a picture through my life.
Cold moon of my duty
To fight the monster in my brain
But soon only beauty
Is all that will remain.

The church is full of infidels
And believers rather shallow
The more I hear, my cold wrath swells,
Their words to make them swallow.
Judge and jury in my head;
Amongst them sits my sin
"Your heart's as black, my friend," said
The Accuser, next to him.
The boon of opportunity
To forgive is too oft vain
But soon only beauty
Is all that will remain.

Bosnian mothers fleeing
Children without food
All that my eyes are seeing
make it hard to see the good.
I'd like to believe that somehow
Somebody somewhere cares

But we'll just turn off our screens now
And go off to bed upstairs.
No room for gratuity
Our hearts can't take the strain
But soon only beauty
Is all that will remain.

16/8/95.

MODERN TIMES

Facebook, Twitter, MSN,
Bebo, Friends Reunited.
Answer, comment, join, reply!
Now you've been invited!!
I've got mail; now I need to send,
I'm even starting a blog.
I'm online so much to just keep up-
I'm even typing in the bog!

I DON'T WANT TO REMEMBER HIM

I don't want to remember him.
How we sat in his kitchen,
his son, my friend and I, with him
over coffee
and laughed until midnight.
I don't want to; not now.

I don't want to remember him.
The night my car broke down,
he came out and towed me back
to his garage. In the pit
we worked until 2am
on that freezing night
until that clutch was fixed.
I don't want to; not now.

I don't want to remember him.
How he laughed and laughed
at my Halloween costume;
A home-made 'Cousin It',
and joined in the fun.
The coolest dad I knew then.
I don't want to; not now.

I don't want to remember him.
How his daughter, in our band,
practising in his attic,
wanted to sing "Oh, Daddy" to him.
I don't want to; not now.
Not now I know what things he did,
in the dark,
to his own children.

5/11/09.

PC

I wish no longer to be known
As politically correct.
I am not a political animal
Nor do I seek to further my own ends.
I am simply
Socionegative terminologically aware.
Nothing more.

For those of my readers,
(Sorry, of course I don't own you)
I mean for the observers of my literature
Who are only non-erudite,
Academically disadvantaged
Or have been scholastically discriminated against,
What I mean is
That I am a smart ass bighead.

Library, University of Ulster, Jordanstown
28/2/96.

WISHES

I wish I was a swing
Hanging on two chains.
Then every backward fling
Would precede a forward gain.

I wish I was a roundabout
With zero self-control.
Pushed in endless circles
Would be not pointless, but my goal.

I wish I was a roller-coaster
Rolling up hill and down slide.
When people would make fun of me
I'd take them for a ride.

I wish I was a dodgem car
Sparking along my track.
If others bumped and hurt me so
I'd simply bump them back.

I wish I was a children's slide
With a surface smooth as glass.
When people tried to sit on me
They'd fall down on their behind.

Playing Fields, Dunmurry
13/6/95.

MARIE

Marie wished.

Wished it so much.

That people would stop saying "This is you. You are this."

Longing to be different, but the night of escape was over. Returning home, sighing,

Marie undressed himself.

SOME HAIKU

Sun beats down on me
Yet the cool breeze is enough
French summer again

Grass in warm sunlight
I lay down on the green ground
Sleep comes easily

Blue betwixt soft clouds
The hill is shadowed, dappled
Slow wind moves them on

Motorway cars pass
I hear the soft birdsong too
Cars don't annoy me

I don't hear bees buzz
Wishing I could stroke one now
I think of honey

Branches, like hard veins
Reach up to the wooing sky
Ending in small leaves

I can't wear my ring
Skin breaks out in itchy sores
Could be worse than this

PLUCKED FROM ABOVE

I saved a bee from drowning
Earlier on today.
The river was calm, but the currents
had gathered the weed 'round the reeds.
The poor thing was clambering all over the weed
up onto the wet reeds,
falling, climbing,
sinking, scrambling,
but drowning.

My hand of salvation
with a dry stick protruded.
The flailing legs
discovered the difference
in the dry hard surface,
and grabbed hard and fast.
It was plucked from above.
I set down the twig
where the creature could dry
and breathe
and recover.

I reached out for it
In empathy,
For I knew its predicament.
Swept by the current
to an alien environment,
crying for something
familiar and dry
to pull it out of its hell.

I looked to my left
to see a brilliant green,
bottle green
crushed damselfly,
A brown and yellow butterfly,
A piece of red
butterfly wing
and a crane fly,
All dead.
Lying twisted
amongst the clotted weed
and debris.

How the many had fallen.
I looked again at the one I had saved.

I must keep my eyes peeled
for that dry stick from above.

Lagan Towpath, Drumbeg
28/2/96.

THE DEAD

Till the resurrection comes
when each shall go to their own end,
The dead shall go on living
simply in our thoughts.

Their life of giving and loving
lingers long and indelible
in the sweet sounds
and enhanced images
of our memory
infused with warmth
imbued with the balm of days
spent wantonly in affection.

But those who lived
in miserly misery and moaning
shall be forgotten
after they are gone
like a bad tooth
once it has fallen
out of the mouth.

Blaris Cemetery
19/8/96.

HEY

Hey
Grey day
Run away
Too long a stay
Now you have no way
To derange and dismay
All the plans for which we prayed
That were steered for in our heyday
And in sunshine and in dreams displayed
Now the noxious ones can no longer say
That we've given up and lost our way
We have fought too long in the fray
Hear no more those who say 'nay'
While the sun shines, make hay
See now our hope's ray
Soon we shall play
And shall say
New day
Hey!

GREYSKY

The grey sky out my window
across the trees,
The rift of clearness between
Reminded me of my surrendered childhood,
Acquiesced to innocence
While we played across the fields,
Through the trees,
Into the bushes,
Oblivious to the clouds threatening
To deluge upon us
and try to spoil our abandon.

The spoiling came late,
After we had mellowed
to a yellower age.
Unaware of the loss,
I returned to the private wood
to see my first adventures
revisited.
Shock, loathing, revulsion
at the sight. Gone
were most of the trees,
the orchards,
the bamboo, hogweed, elephant grass.
All had towered over
our adolescent stature
as that small estate
became a rainforest.

It often did rain,
but the greysky
was miles above the canopy

Where we made shelter
in the bush,
or found shelter
in the derelict mansion
or outhouses.
This was our world;
the outside, above and around
in a different dimension
of space and time
until tea time.

There we played our various games.
Made swings, fell off, climbed the trees
(more than once right to the top).
Lit the bonfires,
and smoked dried hogweed,
(big lads we were!),
our lungs rasping with the sucked-in cinders,
Returning home reeking of smoke,
learning the subtle art
of spinning excuses and yarns to mother.

Time sauntered on.
We grew above the bamboo.
Our hair grew in stranger places.
We found mates, played new games.
Found other ventures, made new shelters,
raised a new brood of innocents.

Unseen,
the bulldozers growled over
our oft-handled
crumbling bricks,
And the dense playground

that was better
than any other made for us.

Now I saw the cleaner,
neater, prettier, more respectable
paths and lawns and flower beds
with benches for us
for when we grow round and stooping and slow.
How smooth,
How mature,
is the City Council Park.

Yet how harsh and stinging
is the greysky I never noticed before,
without the familiar green-brown sanctuary
of leaves and wood and birds and bugs
that had veiled my delicate sight.

The grown-ups never did approve
of that indigenous shade,
the grey more their fashion.

Orangefield Park, Belfast.
1/8/96.

TRAVELLING MAN

The road is calling my soul again;
To walk the serene paths
that whisper my name.
But home gives a warmth
which feels the same.

In the depths of my confusion,
I don't know which to blame:
Is it the haven's chains
or the wild's cries which cause the pain?

18/10/85.

WIND

To fly undaunted into the wind
Must be a wondrous sensation.
To make any headway against its tide
Should give way to elation.

The task of the effort is not to place
Oneself in suspended animation.
But the gaining of mile after yard after inch
Is the adventurer's true vocation.

Loughshore, Jordanstown
10/10/95.

SHOT STAR

My desire was to see a shooting star
Flitting across the moonlit sky
I waited patiently, gazing intently
But none chanced to pass me by.

My endurance weak, my muscles tired
I impelled myself to turn back home
And footsteps dark, my eyes were down
Perusing the road on which I'd roamed.

My journey back was nearly done
The lights of sanctuary glowed ahead
My gaze went up to see the warmth
And in a flash my hopes betrayed.

The tail of a fireball passing out
Of the edge of my disbelieving view
A fleeting glimpse, but not enough
For my soul to see what it wanted to.

How I wish I could be ready
Every single hour of dark
And miss not one of God's great auras
He ordains to last a single spark.

Coleraine
9/8/95.

SOLIDARITY OF INDIVIDUALITY

I know what I am
I know I can do
All the things that I'm meant to do

I know my own strengths
I know all my faults
My shortcomings are not so few

So I don't need someone
To tell right and wrong
In analysis of my behaviour

I have my own conscience
To ring out the warnings
Installed by my only true saviour

It's certainly true
That my outlook on life
Is not shaped by my single eye

For I have enough people
I trust in my life
Whose opinion on which I rely

I'm confident, assured
And draw strength from above
My destiny no other man's making

But I value support
And kinship because…
Well, toughness is usually just faking.

11/1/96.

REASONS FOR SEASONS

The winter snows quickly fall
Then just as swiftly slush and thaw.
The tide of climate warm and cold
Lends not a hand for spell to hold.

And the sun in azure, finds its face
Shuttered by the clouds' embrace.
And blush of heat that seeks to please
Is blown over by a reckless breeze.

Oh, to live in purer climes
In more consistent, seasoned times
Where summer is haze, and winter cold,
Spring is fresh, and autumn gold.

And each day is a foregone thing,
Chance has no place in venturing.
Sky blue blaze or ivory skin
Either to stay 'til day has turned in.

But without variety, life is no fun
And no hint of change can bring tedium.
To learn to live with come what may
Is the truth of the challenge of nature's way.

Lagan Towpath, Drumbeg
18/3/96.

CHEDDARED CHESSBOARD

Those crooks went simply straight ahead
My pick-ups only slanted
The tights jumped over everything
My mean just raved and ranted.

Upon this world of black and white
I keenly played my game
To manoeuvre 'round the obstacles
And intrigue my way to fame.

But the pieces didn't move quite right
With many indiscretions
While the other mean would block my way
And destroy my shrewd intentions.

The other crooks reached my bastion
And flipped over in joy
While their mean devoured the puny prawns
I believed I had to deploy.

I thought the bout was meant to be
Enjoyable but chequered
But now like cheese under the wire
I'm well and truly cheddared.

It seems that as I make my moves
The playing I can bend
But a higher hand which sees the whole
Propels me to my end.

My ego yields eventually glad
To the higher truth which dawns
That my place in design is to happily be
Only king among the prawns.

10/1/96.

WEDDING PRAYER

Pray not this day for peace and blessing,
For it will not last.
Nor ask for the love shown in your eyes
To never die
For it will adjust with the years.
It cannot revert to this,
But with understanding it will evolve.

Pray not this day that you will evade conflict;
You may as well pray
For the wind to stop blowing.
(May the heat of your words
Refine each other's character
And not singe your spirits.)
Nor ask to always win the argument;
Marriage is not a debate
Of opposing views,
But a covenant
Of agreement and accommodation.

But pray for the ability to cast
The harsh words and bad times
Into the vast ocean of dim and distant memory.
And for the wonderful gift
That after the domestic discord
You can look into each other's eyes
And smile
And embrace
And kiss
And laugh out loud
Together.

26/7/96.

EDEN

I lie in green, gentle under my palm
And breathe in the hot and delectable balm
The brilliance of sol, enthroned in the sky
Torching my left cheek and closed eyes.

I open my right to focus and view
Interlacing of white over blue
Spindly gossamer shrouds
Of cotton candy clouds.

I wonder if Eden could have been like this
What else could cause this state of bliss
But the genetic imprint of lost memory
Thin, but present in everything sensory?

The cool night air descends
Diamonds in ebony portend
The beauty that is to come as milk
Poured from the galaxy, gleaming like silk.

Our domain, Metropolis
Has little to do with all of this
Leviathan of man, adverse to nature
Skyscraper idols to his own self-torture.

Trees, birds, wind, flowers, someday I'll see
That all of these joys are all that's to be
New Eden, new Earth, new Heaven combined
In synchronous, hallowed perfection designed.

Giant's Ring, Edenderry & Crawfordsburn
27/7 - 16/8/95.

HE

My parents don't understand me sometimes
But then neither did his sometimes.

I've faced hostility
He did too.

I've had to suffer weddings
Like he did, at least once.

I've spoken to crowds
He knew all about that.

I wondered if they really heard
I wonder if he pondered that.

But crowds aren't what I want
He seemed to tire of them too.

Peace and quiet is vital to my life
He also had that need.

He was rejected
As I have been.

He was misunderstood.
I always have that problem.

He was betrayed.
I do know something of that.

But he had a few close friends.
I thank the Lord for mine.

They did leave him though, when he needed them.
I too have felt alone, though maybe without reason.

I love to walk in gardens and forests.
He spent precious moments in a garden.

I love to sail across a lake
As he had to do at times.

I really like climbing mountains and hills.
He climbed a hill, once too often.

10/8/95.

THE RIVER AND THE RAIN

I went walking by the river.
It had gathered all the rain
That had plunged down for the past five days or so.
Torrential abuse was hurled form the sky
Greyness had multiplied and overrun our spirits
Everything sodden
The fields all small pools
And our socks constantly dank
Stained with the dye of our shoes.
The air still and stale between the spray
No movement to discern.

The memory of the ascent of Donard
On a dripping day the previous week
Was fresh and recountable;
How a cool lunch, hot coffee
Was enjoyed before the climb
Upwards to the saturated mist.
Cloud rolled by and swirled around us
'Til we achieved the plateau
Where wind drove the water through our bones
Over tiny patches of faint white snow
Spied through the haze.

The continual trudge
Through this daylight nightmare scene
Was pure potency of fatigue.
Bu the challenge of the rise
And the vitality of the storm
Lent ardour to our muscle and will.
The top materialised
In the howl of the jaguar wind

Which whipped our torsos to the ground
After our conquest.

The rain there had character
Introduced by the power of the squall
Gusto, bravado, climbing the heights
Of the grassy and heather-bound Mournes.
As had its cousin, dwelling in the Irish mist
Of the bogs and hills of Donegal,
Typically silent and demure enough
To hear the squelch underfoot.
Distilled by the clean Atlantic air
Like a single malt whiskey,
Swelled with fragrance and flavour,
Smooth yet with deep fiery passion.

But this present suburban Belfast troll
Of sogginess could not even qualify
To be either a typhoon or a sweet fuzzy perfume.
All the life, lust and longing
Of a drunk sat on the pavement
Soaked to his skin in his boots.

The river had swelled to the edges of its banks
Brown with mud in its eddies,
Deep, dark and full of the miserable drizzle
Which had run through the hems of my clothes.
I bade farewell, as it carried to sea
All the negative moods of that time.
It could not last forever
And when the sun would shine again
All the bale of gloom and the lumber of woe
Which had lain upon my shoulders
Would be part of the whole

And could yet be moving up the grass of the slopes
And changing to joyful abandon.

Lagan Towpath, Drumbeg
13/1/96.

UNFINISHED

This one's going to be
My 'unfinished' poem.

Then people can stand in awe
and wonder
at what a great poem
it could have been
and so what
a great poem it really is
and

21/10/85.

I GO TO EXTREMES

Living the balance between
decadence and piety.
Traversing the ridge mid
wild abandon and loath apathy,
both careless in their direction.
Walking the precipice of salvation,
Challenging the taunts of the waves below
Yet safe in the surety of my foothold.
That, yes, is life and life to the full.

That grand discipline of moderation
in all things is
Pushing to the limits of restraint,
Not siding with the fashion
of the established way.
Yet the extremes with which
the adventurer touches toes
can be the undoing of the quest.
The quest to be
Neither tenuous
Nor overbearing
Neither timorous
Nor brash,
Neither Dionysian,
Nor stoic,
Neither condemning of innocence
Nor condoning of sin.
Neither too intoxicated
with life's pleasures
Nor completely unimpassioned
by the beauty of this world.

The North wind can blow
the traveller over the south cliff.
That same wind can hold him
up against itself,
leaning over the north cliff,
looking down,
Till one lapse moment
misses the wind's lull,
and he hurtles forth
head downward
To the dashing rocks below.

I shall always tempt my fate
at the edges of existence.
Yet my balance can only grow
better, surer, firmer
With every twist and slip
I have to save myself from.
And I shall remember
that whether I slip off
The East
or the West,
Whether I fall
To my right
or my left,
Either leads to the same end.

31/7/96.

STAIN

People sitting under stained glass
Display a legion of colours.
When the light slips away
They show nought but grey.
Why can't the tones of each soul
Radiate out its own tune?

Singular hue
Cannot make a picture,
But a run of all dyes
Is a fever of thunder clouds.
Yet when red borders blue
And black verges green,
A mosaic is cast
By their contrasting shades.

Metropolitan Tabernacle, Whitewell.
26/11/95.

FALL

The dead, dried up leaf
Fell before my eyes.
It twirled and swirled
like a burst paper bag,
Its stalk spiralling
Quite quickly.
Its body
encompassing itself
again and again.
For a few seconds only.
Then with deft silent flop,
the dervish
stopped on the water.
A solitary ripple
marked its final act.

Strange
How beautiful
could be this plain
nothing.
Not even the bobbing, prancing flies
so unmistakably alive
Could flitter a dance so precise
Above the river.
Could never weave their gauze
in unity
Nor fly so straight and true.

Lagan Towpath, Drumbeg
19/9/96.

LAVENDER DAY

The sky was lavender haze
Spring was creeping over the roof
I entered the building.

Upon the hardened stairs
A girl walked before me, aloof
Lavender perfume trailing.

There was time to kill that morning
And again in the noontime lull
When usually that day was a squeeze.

My thoughts were bathed in praying
An aeon ran around in my skull
And I wished for an aura of ease.

I could see no purpose by daytime
No reason for soon-coming night
And my future seemed so very bleak.

But just what I needed was slack time
To travail for a friend in their plight
When my own troubled spirit was weak.

The lavender mist is still here
Shrouding the city and hills
"A strange hue," I remark in my mind.

I should not have hearkened to fear
I know serendipity kills
All the problems my soul tries to find.

University of Ulster, Jordanstown, 19/3/96.

SUN

Stage centre
The sun enters
Its private amphitheatre.

Its rays of amber
Supporting the canopy
Of gathering blue.

Streams of honey
Pour down to the event
Welcoming the maker of their hue.

Golden dome ascends
And creeps intangibly
But inexorably upwards
And slightly to the right,
That titanic mass of fire
On its diurnal round of heaven
As has been done
Since it was flung into its place
In space
With all her sundry sisters.

Hazelbank, Belfast Lough.
11/12/95.

THOUGHTS

I thought that love was natural
But I learnt that it was hard work

I thought that life was for the taking
But I learnt that my life was for sharing

I thought that happiness was to be sought
But I learnt by being still that it sought me

I thought that I would want others' company
But I was amazed to learn that they would want mine

I thought that I would covet solitude
But I learnt that true fellowship was the greater quest

I thought that friends would be there forever
But I learnt that I could lose them through neglect

I thought that I had to make my universe fit me
But I learnt that the universe was made for me to fit into

I thought that parenthood would be fun
But I learnt

I thought that I knew most things
But I learnt that most of the things
I thought I knew
Were only half the truth
Of what I ought to know.

I learnt that the sum

Of what there is yet to learn
Over what I have learnt so far
Is infinity.
Nay, it is eternity.

Eternity, I embrace thee.

5/11/96.

MOUNTAIN OF TESTING

The ice can spike and the wind can shrill
But a walk in their face can still be a thrill,
If only I push on through at my will
And reach the bliss where their temper is still.

Or at least to the summit while their fevers still rage,
And elation of conquest is tenacity's wage:
Though the gale may still howl, victory will assuage
And the descent transcribe to a different page.

18/3/96.

WHY?

Why should I want to explain things?
Why not keep it locked up inside?
Why find an ear that wants to hear?
Why someone in whom to confide?

Why are so many unwilling?
Why do they not wish to share?
Why not give relief to their own pent-up grief?
Why pretend they don't really care?

Why are men made to feel feeble?
Why tell them they're not meant to cry?
Why is emotion taboo in expression?
Why chastised, who attempt to try?

Why is our present 'individualist' culture
So succumbing to this golden rule?
Why does 'care in the community'
Mean nought but political wool?
Why is the pretence of independence
To stand on one's own two feet?
Why can one not be individual
And with true friends be made complete?

Lambeg
1/1/96.

LAW OF RETURN

My freedom is not unfettered
while other remain bound.

My wealth does not luxuriate
unless apportioned with those in need.

My possessions mean nothing
unless I learn that they are unimportant.

My salvation is but selfish
until I share it with other souls.

I can only find forgiveness
when I give it freely.

The love I have come to know in my life
must be requited to survive.

My friends are there for me
because I am there for them.

But my Lord is there for me
because he is.

13/8/96.

COMEDY LIMERICKS
(I won a small prize from the BBC for these)

To Dibley there came a plump vicar,
Felt that some folk there couldn't be sicker.
"But they're friendly," thought she,
"And I think they like me."
'Til they built a big man out of wicker!

I Manuel, I a waiter, I say "qué?"
Missa Fawty says I make him turn grey!
I say "qué?" once again,
Then I feel a sharp pain!
He hitta me on the head with a tray!

UNVEILING

The mountains held up the mist
all week long.
Shy brides fitting their veils
at mirrors,
Excited by encroach of the time
of unveiling.
Teasing out an eye or two
to look up
Once or twice, no more
and let it down again,
or drop it down their whole length.

And the floss would lift
at times,
Roll back to show the way
they were baiting
Me out of my senses,
waiting
For the uncovering
of their beauty.

We drove along the potted, hummocking
and sheen-black veins,
Varicose in the deepest green
sea of grass
and waves of hedge.
Sometimes the sky leaked.
The white-smoke trails
above the green tops
moved and swirled
But the Christmas cotton carpet

kept the faces
of the maidens hidden.
Each hungry glance
out the window
went unserved,
Even past supper.

The morning we packed was chilled
and distilled
like the clearest of ice.
I threw off my quilt
then gathered it back
to ward off the evil freeze.

Too late.
It was knotwork
around my limbs.
Scurrying across the caravan floor,
a hamster through its cage,
I struck the matches
to nurture flame from the gas.
Then
Opening the curtains,
Gasping left my breast
at the sight:
The ladies of the range
had dropped their arms
to cover their ivory bodies,
Spreading their ivory covers
across the valley floor.

MacGillycuddy's Reeks
3/9/96.

65

THE SECRET LANGUAGE

Two may know and see as they meet
That words can't express what they want to admit.
To voice their emotion would be inadequate
For their hearts paint in oils inarticulate
Which none but the two could ever interpret
But evaluation is not a prerequisite.

Maybe someday they can express the secret
In exchanges rather more concrete
Until that time their voices remain quiet
Or their work of art they would simply annihilate.

22/7/95.

PROMISE REGRESSED

How what love I had left so quickly turned
Into hatred and spurious passion that burned
My soul to a crisp, with a wanton to kill
That others can say, but do not know the thrill

Of how I could feel and see so clear,
My fingers around your throat, watch your fear,
As I would end your life and drop your corpse
And walk away calmly; smiling, of course.

BRIDGE THAT I BURNT

(Inspiration from "Nails in my Feet" by Crowded House)

Bring me some water
For the burning bridge.
I need some water
For my burning bridge.
I embarked on the crossing
My gait a little too firm
My mind thought it out
But my spirit did not leap to confirm.

I failed to see,
Did not look ahead
And now on an island
My cold feet tread.
I can't stand the thought,
Will not face a future
So bleak on a rock
On a bland ocean sombre.

I wish to return
To set off elsewhere
Upon the true quest
That my life wants to share.
But can someone come
And quench now the fire?
The structure is crumbling
Too much to retire.

I suppose that I'm now
Resigned to my fate.
Why I should be here
I can't answer yet.

How my steps brought me
I know only too well.
Though as always
The lesson of time will tell.

I'll watch the horizon
For the water to bring,
The one that I cried to,
Some water to bring.
Their ship at the shore
Of my being will tether
To land and to touch
Then to sail off together.

4/9/95.

OBSERVATIONS

DEFINITION OF PURPOSE

Acceptance is understanding
how events have brought you here,
but maybe not why.

Resignation is the realisation of
why circumstances have conspired to put you there,
but not necessarily how.

But compromise is neither here nor there.

31/5/95.

LOVE & LIFE

Summer is not summer without strawberries.
Winter is not winter without snow.
And love is not love without commitment;
Cannot proclaim what its conduct does not show.

Triumph is not achieved without endeavour.
Birth is not accomplished without pain.
And life's not just a slide down a merry fairground ride;
With no trying times, there is no forward gain.

6/7/96.

SHALOM

Happiness without contentment
is a yacht becalmed in blissful weather
when you'd rather be at the shore.

Contentment without happiness
is sailing safely through the storm
knowing the shore is in sight.

Neither is realising you're lost at sea.

But both is seeing the coastline,
then peacefully steering the boat
the other way.

6/7/96.

THE HIGH PLACE REVISITED

Hush! A Silence
So much colder
than my pounding heart,
Yet more warmhearted
than the wind
Which till then had howled
across my ears.

Rounding the summit tor
of tensile rock monumentally dense
Saw the end of the barrage
Of harsh northeaster,
Moaning over the top
Like one forsaken banshee
bent on revenge.
My T-shirt no longer rippled
to its voice
but hung betwixt sack-straps
limp and damp
with mist and hard-earned sweat.

Now
Only the footfall
of sheep
and munch
of grass
Could be discerned.
Even the rock
seemed to creak
with age.
My breath,

which had been lost to the wind,
the sight would not restore.
Breaking from the cloud,
the long green distance
of fields and walls and water
Met the horizon
in perfect coalescence
of peace.

My companion
went to find
A cove for dealing lunch
of warm tea and grub.

Yet I withstood my stomach, for a moment,
To inhale the aroma of freedom
That silence had bequeathed.
And thought,
for a moment,
That I could sit down
right here
right now
atop my conquest
and never eat again
and die a happy man.

Slieve Binnian, Mourne Mountains
21/9/96.

MIRROR

Silver reflects more than white.
It mirrors to perfection.
White just blurs a commotion.
White noise. Silver silence.

White is a garment
Worn by those to declare their purity.
Silver is a quality
Bequeathed by the fire which refines.

The bone that clubs the head
Is made out of white
But the sword which pierces hearts
In silver is forged.

To blanch myself to white
Is an act futile and vain
For the substance of my being
Has not altered.

But to shine like furnaced silver
Needs the work of a master
To mould the masterpiece
Of integrity and perfection.

11/1/96.

[This has kindled thoughts within me again which shall be
incorporated into 'The Obsidian Way of Jesus'!]

WASP

Little wasp, annoying wasp,
Buzzing 'round my head.
A magazine! I roll it up
And swing it. SPLAT! You're dead.

21/9/95.

REAL REALITY

Reality fades while you sleep
And the nightmares and dreams shall keep
Your attention from the crisscross logic
Of the web spun by your tragic
Heed of fantasy wish and fear.

Then the waking brings the dawning
That all that was, was screening
Out the truth of how your living
Can be so unforgiving
When you can't control the things you see and hear.

And phantasm can blind you
But daylight will remind you
That this world with its worries
Is firmer than the flurries
Of the tinctures in the shadows of your mind.

That which passes is the spectre
What will last is the protector
Of the things your heart discerns
To be of value, as it learns
To cling to any life that it may find.

But for all our lives will do and see
Where really is reality?
The filling of our gut
And the lining of our nest;
Is this the soul's adventure
Or the intellect's great quest?

Beyond the pale vision
Of our life's condition
There must be a waking
Which leads to forsaking
All bogus musing
This world is confusing
With wisdom and merit
Which means to inherit
That which decays
With the passing of days
As images of the night
Evaporate in the light.

14/12/95.

THE SEA AND ME

The sea that goes around the world
Has come back again today.
To all the other shores she's shingled
I wish she'd carry me away.

She slithers daily down the beach
Yet returns to it in waves.
So feminine, she can't decide:
I can't grasp how she behaves.

If I had the chance to run away
I presume I might just go.
But stronger ties of loyalty
Form the only way I know.

The dichotomy of what I want
In life is always there;
To divulge and do just what I want
Or to yield and humbly serve.

To yield is often portrayed
As a soft and feminine trait,
But the greatest man did yield his life
To a painful, shameful fate.

My thoughts will always be plagued
By the doubts and fears of life.
My walk will follow all the roads
Of both victory and strife.

I am just like the ocean
In all her ebbs and flows

And the even keel that I like
Is lost in my toss and throws.

I suppose I'm not the man
I'd really like to believe
But in me is a man
In whom I can believe.

Loughshore, Jordanstown
28/2/96.

EPILOGUE

Art is art and crap is crap
And ne'er the twain shall meet.
If the critics compare my art with crap
I'll wipe their words from off my feet.
But if you, lay reader, think my work is crap
By all means, please toss it in the street.

Library, University of Ulster, Jordanstown.
16/4/96.

BYE

My friend said goodbye to his son.

"Drive careful, son!"

"Awk, Da!!"

Printed in Great Britain
by Amazon